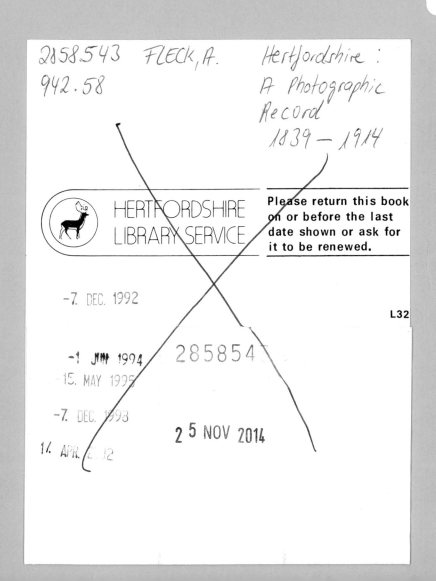

# HERTFORDSHIRE

## A PHOTOGRAPHIC RECORD
### 1839–1914

Alan Fleck

# HERTFORDSHIRE

A PHOTOGRAPHIC RECORD
1839–1914

## Alan Fleck

COUNTRYSIDE BOOKS

NEWBURY, BERKSHIRE

First Published 1989
© Alan Fleck 1989

COUNTRYSIDE BOOKS
3 Catherine Road
Newbury, Berkshire

ISBN 1 85306 058 5


Designed by Mon Mohan

Produced through MRM Associates Ltd., Reading
Printed in England

# Contents

Thomas Benwell Latchmore, 1832–1908. The son of a Quaker grocer in Hitchin, Latchmore capitalised on the carte-de-visite boom of the 1860s, but prospered as a studio and landscape photographer. Travelling widely in Hertfordshire when neither travel nor photography were easy, he left an archive of several thousand prints. Many of them appear in this book.

# Foreword

Provincial museums have changed a lot since I was a boy. Forty years ago the contents of those that I knew consisted mainly of stuffed birds, stuffed animals, stuffed fish, cabinets of birds' eggs and fossils and a few rusty bygones, the most exciting of which was an ancient man-trap. Nowadays they are far more interesting places and one reason for this is the way the more enlightened curators have been able to create the right ambience for their displays by making excellent use of early photographs. Take fashions, for instance; Victorian crinolines mounted on dummies are one thing – but place them in front of a huge enlargement of a photograph of ladies wearing similar clothes at a garden party in the 1850s and the exhibits almost come to life.

The museum curator Alan Fleck, who compiled this book, was one of the first to make good use of the work of Hertfordshire's pioneer photographers in this way. At Hitchin Museum, with colleagues past and present, he has also been responsible for restoring what I believe to be the county's most comprehensive collection of Victorian photographs. This was the work of T.B. Latchmore who used his cameras to obtain a wonderful record of town and village life in Hertfordshire during the second half of the 19th century but whose vast collection of original photographic plates was destroyed in the 1940s. In the last few years, however, Alan has managed to trace and re-photograph a great many examples of Latchmore's early work which, fortunately, had survived in the form of prints kept by local families or in scrap books and other material donated to his museum. We have good reason to be grateful to him for the work he has done to ensure the preservation of this most important photographic record of our county's history.

So, although other photographers across the county are well-represented, it is not surprising that it is the work of Latchmore that forms the nucleus of this book from which, with the help of good factual captions and introductions, we are able to learn much about the work of our pioneer cameramen and of the people and places that became the first subjects to face the camera's lens.

*RICHARD WHITMORE*
Hitchin 1989

# Introduction

The invention of photography was revolutionary in more ways than one. Not only was it a miraculous scientific attainment, instantly purloined by artists for their own ends, but also a new form of documentation, through which many could see and interpret what had hitherto been the preserve of the few. Thus many could now see the true faces of the royal family, aristocrats, gentry and politicians, who before had been depicted only in line drawings, engravings or lithographs, with all the attendant distortions, whether intentional or not.

Photography was initially the preserve of the wealthy. Fox Talbot himself, the inventor of the calotype, photographed the buildings and many of his staff at Lacock Abbey, but once the process itself had spread beyond the small circle of inventors, scientific advisers, wealthy enthusiasts and patrons to become commercially available, it not unnaturally appealed mostly to those able to afford the high prices charged for the finished product. The earliest photographs tend therefore to depict the wealthy.

Landscape photography grew up closely related to this trend. The wealthy owned and farmed the land through their tenants, and wished to depict it and their development of it through the new medium, just as landowners had done in the 18th century through portraiture – an exhibition of their own skills and status. The early photographers recognised both this wish and their own need to advertise their new-found artistry.

This was certainly true of Thomas Benwell Latchmore, for example. During the 1850s, while helping his parents in their grocery shop in Hitchin High Street, Benwell developed an interest in photography. Starting with the daguerreotype, he followed and mastered the early processes of photography, and in June 1864 opened his first portrait studio in what was then Bancroft Street. His studio was in part of the house of a friend, the schoolmaster William Dawson, but it is clear that Latchmore was enjoying the patronage and financial assistance of the Society of Friends, or Quakers. From the start Benwell advertised photographs of local views for sale, and over his lifetime he built up what is arguably the best Victorian topographical record of the county.

Frederick Downer opened his studio in Watford in 1862, following a generally similar path. He concentrated on portrait photography, and soon extended this specialisation to include the gentry in their country homes just outside London – homes growing in number as the advantages of rail transport were appreciated.

The mid-1860s saw a sudden craze for small photographic portraits the size of visiting cards, which came to be known as cartes-de-visite. This craze could not have come at a better time for the Latchmores and Downers, for it guaranteed a steady income and enabled them to consolidate their new businesses and diversify their trade. The craze itself forced prices down and by so doing changed the pattern of photographic portraiture. No longer was it the prerogative of the rich. From 1863 to 1866 the cost of a single carte-de-visite in Hitchin dropped from 15p to around 6p, the equivalent of £1.30 today. By way of simple comparison, one could buy a gallon of ale for 7p or a lady's silk umbrella for 45p, and a domestic cook might earn £14 per year, bed and board included. Photographers' subjects were no longer the aristocrat and the wealthy, but the shop-keeper and the domestic servant too.

Competition was not restricted to portrait photography. Landscape views fell in price too, and became popular, foreshadowing the later rise of the postcard. In this competitive market, photographers did not necessarily specialise; Downer attempted to diversify into newspaper production, only to be cast down by the First World War and the attendant shortage of newsprint. Latchmore to a limited extent sub-contracted for Francis Frith & Co., the photographic publishers of Reigate, and his son Thomas William went on to publish postcards on his own account, and later moved into wedding photography.

From very tentative beginnings, photography moved into a mass market. Not surprisingly, many of the better images became connoisseur items and collectors' pieces, ultimately finding their way thence into museums, where they remain for the enjoyment of all. Most reached museums through private individuals generous to pass them into public care: if you care too, do consult your local museum on the best way to store and display these fragile historical records. Museums in Hertfordshire contain their share of portrait, landscape and documentary photographs, and the aim of this book is quite simply to reveal some of the best of those pictures and afford them a wider public.

I am grateful to Mrs. K. L. Murray, Mr. Bill Smith and my colleagues in Hertford, Letchworth First Garden City, Luton, Royston, St. Albans and Watford Museums for the use of photographs from their collections in this book.

Alan Fleck

# The Land

The land is the ultimate resource. Without it, none can survive. We are born from it, live off its plants and animals, and ultimately return to it. The farmer is the ultimate provider, the figure upon whom we all depend for our daily bread.

Hertfordshire is primarily an agricultural county, notable for its lack of heavy industry. It has been linked to grain industries since the medieval period, growing wheat and barley, milling, malting, and brewing. The northern and eastern parts of the county saw a flourishing wool trade until the 17th century, though this was largely because those areas of the county were crossed by the Chilterns, which made agriculture difficult, or because economic circumstances at the time made sheep more profitable. Sir Henry Chauncy, in his *Historical Antiquities of Hertfordshire* commented in 1700:

> 'most of the Meadows are dry; the Hills wet and cold, for they are Clay, therefore barren; and for divers Parts it contains Chalk within a Foot or a Fathom of the Surface of the Ground, which enables the industrious Farmer, after the great Charges in Compost and Tillage, to force from thence excellent Wheat and Barley, with good Oats and Pease . . .'

Chauncy clearly felt that improvements were being made, by those with the power to force the earth to yield forth her increase, and those too who were industrious enough to make the effort. In the 18th century there were several writers analysing current farming practices, and one such was of course William Ellis of Little Gaddesden. *The Practical Farmer, or, The Hertfordshire Husbandman* contained many 'new Improvements in Husbandry', ways of improving soil, discussions of the virtues of foreign wheats, and a comparison of different methods of farming in different counties.

To the average farm labourer, all this meant little. Life was much the same as it had been for his father, and his father too. The advent of mechanisation was sporadic, and failure still more frequent than success, but sheer effort could be brought by steam. Steam could pull a plough, could drive a threshing engine, could make a few labourers redundant and thereby lose them their homes. Those who adapted to it and survived were relieved of some of their more onerous tasks. The advent of the reaper-binder in the 1880s speeded up the harvest enormously – again at a cost in human terms. For those who lost their jobs and tied cottages, it might mean a job in a factory, such as Thomas Perkins' factory in Hitchin. Perkins made ploughs and agricultural steam engines, and went on to found what was to become Perkins Diesel.

Ploughing by steam at Willian, 1900. Steam ploughing had great advantages where fields were large and the land fairly flat – it thrived in Lincolnshire. It required few men, and the equipment could be hired with its operatives, and it put scant load upon the soil, unlike a modern tractor. A ploughing engine at each side of the field pulled a multiple-gang plough back and forth between them on a cable as they worked their way up the headland.

Reaping by hand, Barley. An onerous task, wearying and repetitive; the rare breaks were for sharpening the scythes and for beer provided by the farmer by the barrel. Such was the effort of the job that few became inebriated, though the quantity consumed might be considerable.

Reaper-binder cutting beans, Barley, around 1912. The reaper-binder was the invention of Cyrus McCormick, an American who displayed his reaper at the Great Exhibition of 1851. Its appearance did not go unremarked, and at the Royal Show of 1863, 45 different brands of reaper were on show. By the 1880s the binding mechanism had been incorporated and the design was scarcely altered until the arrival of the first combine harvesters just before the Second World War.

Steam threshing at Lilley, around 1914. The threshing set – traction engine,
threshing engine and box van for the men – was hired in much the same way as the
steam plough. Since the threshing machine needed a man to feed the stooks in
from the top, he had to stand up there, catching forksful and feeding them into the
drum behind him. One false step and his leg was threshed too. Wooden legs were
not uncommon amongst farm workers . . .

Threshing a stack at Therfield, around 1914. Threshing was never much fun, and this photograph depicts it on a cold winter's day. Several of the men are wearing 'yarks', strings tied around their trouser-legs to keep out bugs and small rodents. The day's work is done – hence the lounging against the stationary engine – and a cover has been put over the threshing machine.

Milling at Ickleford around 1885. The miller peeps out of the window while the omnipresent small boys gape at the photographer.

Sheep on kale, Barley, around 1904. The shepherd with his crook keeps a watchful eye, while the very neatly attired farmer, Clear Wilkerson, surveys all.

When the day's work was done, there was often time to wander down to the local tavern for a jar of the local brew – often totally local, brewed on the premises by mine host and his wife, though by the 19th century this was rapidly dying out. Here at the White Lion in Walkern a group of workers, some in the smocks, enjoy a pint.

Thomas Perkins' staff, Bancroft, Hitchin. These men stand in front of stationary
engines, which had to be pulled by horse-power to the site, while traction engines
were self-propelled. Perkins was a great advocate of steam ploughing and entered
his products in many competitions, pointing out the economic advantages 'the cost
of the ploughing which we had seen done by the 8-horse engine set, amounting to
7 shillings per acre . . . I have since done a calculation of doing the same work by
horses, showing that it would amount to 12/6 per acre.'

# Transport

Perhaps because of the county's proximity to London, there had already grown up a strong trade in various commodities – straw and hay in for the capital's horses, soot and rags out for land treatment, and grain of various kinds in, both for bread and for brewing. Traditionally, goods had been moved by wagon or pack horse on roads little cared for since the collapse of the Roman empire – sloughs of despond in winter and bruisingly hard in a dry summer. The growth of the canal movement in the 18th century had a considerable impact for Ware, Hertford and Watford; all these towns had substantial brewing and malting industries, and the canals obviously benefited their London trade directly.

The blacksmith, the farrier and the wheelwright were the basic manufacturers of transport equipment, resident in all but the smallest hamlets since roads maintained their importance for local trade. The carter and the waggoner were just as important economically, maintaining a regular goods distribution network on a larger scale – perhaps over a 20 mile radius – but have never achieved the same public esteem as the craftsmen who maintained their vehicles.

The steam engine, invented to pump water out of coal mines, was soon miniaturised for railway use, and Hertfordshire was steadily webbed over with new lines. The London & North Western Railway opened in 1837, the Great Eastern was complete to Bishops Stortford by 1842 and the Great Northern to Peterborough by 1850. The Midland opened in 1839, but only as far south as Leicester; it opened a branch south to Hitchin in 1857 and shared the Great Northern lines to King's Cross, finally opening a line to St Pancras in 1868. The development of these lines was undertaken through private venture capital, generally with considerable success. Many more lines were planned than ever were built – between 1834 and 1902, 2,228 miles were planned in Hertfordshire, but only 721 were built – but even so, the very multiplicity of lines built led to problems. The interfacing of different companies' timetables and the frequent sharing of lines often led to much delay.

The spread of the bicycle at first as a leisure item, and later as a cheap form of short-range transport, had its own effect both on pubs, which advertised their facilities for cyclists, and for local shops, retailing and repairing the hardware. Clubs sprang up to cater for groups, so the bicycle had a social value too. The members of these clubs ranged over a vast area: day trips from the north of the county to London and back were quite common.

The motor car was to spread more slowly. It was expensive to buy and required great expertise to maintain, making it initially the preserve of the wealthy. Like the bicycle, it too had an initial cult following, and in some areas still does! It had some advantages over the horse, which required feeding even when not in use and had to be caught and harnessed. The internal combustion engine required a fuel which had to be imported, but the range of the vehicle was unlimited, giving it great potential for light transport work. The early bus was to encourage the growth of the motor industry through its use in the First World War and, of course, the exactly parallel decline of the wheelwright, blacksmith and farrier.

Blacksmith's shop at Essendon, around 1865. The blacksmith repaired any ferrous metal item not made by casting, so was an essential though not obvious component of the transport system. While the wheelwright and the wagon-builder were the initial constructors, it was down to the blacksmith to do running repairs on the metal fittings of vehicles, as well as making all manner of domestic and agricultural equipment – such as the fencing visible here.

Bulk loads had to be moved across country by horse-power. The gradual improvements in road conditions, through the work of Telford, MacAdam and, occasionally, the Turnpike Trusts, led to a move away from the pack horse in favour of the wagon. A horse could carry 50 kilos on its back and pull 500 kilos in a cart or wagon. Since the same horse could shift 50 tonnes at a steady speed in a canal barge, it is not surprising that the canal system expanded. Here, a wagon carrying grain waits outside the pub at North Mimms.

'Mr Kirtley's Engine Design, built by E.B. Wilson & Co., Leeds'. The style of the dresses indicates a date squarely on the Midland Railway's presence in Hitchin, 1858 until 1865, and the locomotive is standing outside the old Midland shed at Hitchin, demolished only a week or so before this text was written.

Royston Station in the 1890s. Photographers were very keen on depicting the high-tech of the day in the form of the latest designs of railway engine, and it is not common to find such a low-key photograph as this – just the rear of the train.

Stevenage Station, around 1880. The original Stevenage Station was obviously built in 1850 to coincide with the opening of the Great Northern Railway, and this photograph clearly shows a group of buildings architecturally closely akin to Hitchin Station. It was, however, later rebuilt, ultimately to be demolished after a station on a different site was opened in 1973 to cater for the expanding new town.

Stevenage Station, around 1910, after it had been rebuilt on a much larger scale, and with a greater architectural unity. The two horses were used for shunting.

While the Victorian railway network was certainly expansive, it was not omnipresent, and goods had to be distributed throughout the hinterland of the rail head. The railways themselves usually maintained a fleet of horse-drawn wagons of various kinds, and the Royal Mail did too. This Parcel Mail van is making a delivery in a north Hertfordshire village: Mr Beech at the right-hand edge appears in a group photograph of the Hitchin Post Office staff in 1895.

Early cycling was very much a social and group activity before it evolved to a form of mass transport. Arthur Latchmore founded a cycle club at the Woodlands School in Hitchin in 1875. A year later, his brother photographed the club in the school yard. These of course were the sons of well-to-do traders, each with an 'ordinary' bicycle costing perhaps 10 guineas, equivalent to around £250 today. The safety bicycle, with two equal sized wheels, did not appear until the 1880s.

The early motor car had exactly the same coterie of followers as the early bicycle; they just had to be wealthier. The vehicles afforded little protection from the weather if inclement and from dust, grit and flies on those unending Edwardian 'summer' days. The ladies took to wearing hats with veils, though some wore goggles or even a silk hood with a mica eyepiece. This hardy rally is about to set off from Hexton Manor, in 1905.

Hitchin bus rank in Hermitage Road. Early photographs of buses seem hard to come by, especially for the northern part of the county. This one was taken in 1923, but is the earliest datable photograph available. The buses ran regular services over quite long routes – those in this photograph indicate Pirton, 4 miles from Hitchin, and Meppershall, about 10 miles. There was also a service via Offley Hill to Luton, though this route had its problems in the winter if the roads were icy: the able-bodied passengers were expected to get out and push.

Other informal networks of road transport existed too, in the form of carters. These men and women made regular scheduled runs from town to town, passing through various villages on the route. Goods ordered to a railhead or from shops in large towns would be collected and brought back: they might help out in times of adversity, too, for one Hitchin lady recalls as a child returning from a tonsillectomy operation on the carter's cart! This is Mrs Malyon, a carter from Buckland to Royston, outside the Boar's Head in Royston around 1866.

# The Big House

A little place in the country was the ideal of many a Victorian family, but only those who had amassed or acquired considerable wealth were ever able to attain it. Large houses need large supporting staffs, and themselves require continual maintenance.

None the less, there were many who, through inheritance or through industry, were able to support such establishments. Some were born to country houses, some achieved country houses, and some, like the clergy even today, had country houses thrust upon them.

Some country houses are not houses at all, but small palaces, and are nationally known as such. Hatfield attained palatial opulence as early as 1608; Knebworth was a large house dating from around 1500, demolished in 1811 and rebuilt as 'a romantic paraphrase of a Gothic palace' as Pevsner terms it, from 1815. But these large houses were only the most obvious part of a continuous spectrum, from Buckingham Palace down to the meanest hovel. In between lived the aristocracy, the industrialists, the landed gentry, the clergy.

With the development of the railway networks out of London, many new country houses were built. The financially adept of the metropolis were then able to indulge their fantasies for country living – at least until the suburban expansion of the capital washed around them. As time went on, different fates befell these houses, just as befell their owners. Some, like Ickleford Manor, burnt down. Many, like Hartsbourne Manor House in Bushey Heath, have already been demolished for redevelopment; others, like Hitchin Priory, have retired from family life after a few centuries to become the offices of firms themselves fleeing the capital. The vast majority have kept themselves to themselves, changing hands from time to time, occasionally accreting a new wing or a conservatory, or subsiding into genteel decay, to be restored by a new Prince Charming as national finances ebb and flow.

Photographs of the big houses reveal not only the scale of some of the houses but also the broad outlines of the lives that were led in them – lives led at a leisurely pace, playing games, collecting, reading. Many of these activities we take as characteristic of people with money, and it is necessary to bear in mind the other side of the coin and look at the urban squalor where others lived. For these, a life of service in 'the big house' was escape, release from squalor.

Mrs Anna Baker, left, and friends at Bayfordbury, outside Hertford, 1852–1856. William Robert Baker inherited the substantial Bayfordbury estate when he was but 14 years old, direct from his great-grandfather, who had bought it in 1757. In 1835 William Robert became one of the youngest men ever to be appointed High Sheriff of the County, aged only 25. The same year he began a series of improvements to the property, developing the garden and adding a pinetum. Here his wife Anna entertains Sir Bootle and Lady Boothby, and an unidentified young woman.

William Robert Baker became interested in photography in the 1830s, while photography was still a secret in the hands of its inventors. He took many photographs in Europe while on the Grand Tour, but recorded work on his own estate, such as this calotype view of the facade of the house, with a specimen monkey-puzzle tree, dating probably from the 1840s.

Hartsbourne Manor House, Bushey Heath. Ladies practising archery between 1869 and 1874. The house has now been demolished for redevelopment. Archery was a popular sport for ladies since it was not unduly active and therefore needed no great concessions to dress.

Hartsbourne Manor House, Bushey Heath. The interior of a gentleman's house was not only a status symbol in itself, but its contents and their arrangement indicated his particular interests. A look at the contents of this room reveals a lot about the house's owner. He wishes us to know of his interest in sport – from the antlers on the right and the stuffed game birds, of his interest in culture – from the apparently oriental vases on pedestals, and in the history of his own family – most of the paintings are portraits.

While the house was an advertisement for the owner's achievements and interests, this did not mean that the needs (or presumed needs) of the ladies were neglected. They often had their own dressing and withdrawing rooms as here again in Hartsbourne, where a lady sits reading in a thoroughly feminine room. While it may appear ornate, it appears also to suffer from a leaky roof in the top left corner.

Charles Cholmeley Hale and family at Kingswalden, 1880–1884. Here the ladies are dressed for more active pursuits – the girls for riding and the young ladies for tennis. The Hales lived at Kingswalden until the death of Charles Cholmeley (at the back, leaning against the window) in 1884. Educated at Eton, Charles had served in the Second Battalion, The Rifle Brigade in Canada and South Africa, and succeeded to the family home in 1852 when he was 22.

Mrs Prime with a friend in the garden of The Hermitage, Hitchin, around 1866. Charles E. Prime was usually described simply as a 'gentleman', and he was noted for his activity in pursuit of the fox. 'I was asked to be the treasurer of the hunt, and when Col. Lionel Ames died, I became the secretary of the Hunt club also. I have besides meddled in steeple-chasing and racing . . . I believe I leave the county with the friendship of all the gentlemen I know, and I hope and believe with the friendship of all the farmers I know . . .'

Croquet party on the lawn. Hitchin Priory, around 1868. Frederick Peter Delmé Radcliffe leans on his stick, left, next to his wife who perches not quite comfortably on a garden chair. After the Dissolution of the Monasteries Hitchin Priory was purchased by Ralph Radcliffe in 1548 as a school. His successors slowly increased in wealth until John Radcliffe, a trader in the Levant, commissioned Robert Adam in 1770 to build a country house. The mansion beggared Radcliffe, but family fortunes had recovered by 1868.

Ickleford Manor, around 1905. In 1851 this Georgian house was run by a cook, a nurse, a housemaid, nurserymaid, kitchenmaid, butler, head gardener, footman, page and groom. The sale catalogue in February 1919 described two miles of excellent trout fishing, 300 acres of rough shooting, a well timbered park, a long carriage drive and picturesque lodge, halls, four reception rooms, 16 bedrooms, two bathrooms, central heating, stabling, acetylene gas, etc. etc. Later in 1919 the house burnt down, and it was never rebuilt.

# Towns

Many of the county's towns are medieval in origin like Hertford, Watford, or Royston packed with small streets, while others grew out of villages and had greatness thrust upon them later, such as Welwyn, Stevenage or Letchworth. A century and a half ago, the disparity between towns was far less, their similarities more obvious. Many had specific features in common: market towns tended towards a similar plan, with the market street often fossilising in the medieval period as a long spindle shape of buildings, sometimes to such a width that the edges become streets in their own right. Later, towns on coaching routes, like Watford and Hitchin, sprouted inns with stabling behind, and carriage-arches for access – a far more elaborate structure than a village pub. There was obviously no need of by-passes; traffic automatically headed for the town centre, even if double-parking of carts caused a problem, and buildings were occasionally demolished to ease traffic flow.

Towns managed to survive through being relatively self sufficient. They contributed to the main stream of county or regional life, but were by no means the sole providers. Thus Baldock and Ware malted and brewed, Hitchin tanned and yielded lavender, while Watford made paper and printed upon it. Still others just missed the boat – Hitchin quite literally, failing to join the canal network on a spur from the Ivel, and having its dreams of becoming a railway centre usurped by Derby at the outset of the First World War.

The inhabitants had common needs, and particular crafts satisfied them. As time went on, those needs changed, or the craft technology changed. Where a farrier, ostler or wheelwright once worked, now stands a petrol station. Where a craftsman carved wood, filed metal or slit leather, now stands a factory. Such progress, or development, has both its vices and its virtues.

Mass production has led to uniformity in more than just the means of manufacture, and has led to a self-consciousness of non-uniformity. Just look at a suburban housing estate, and merely a door of a different paint colour may offend. But there is virtue in diversity. We can see only too clearly that Old Stevenage High Street is 'different' from New Stevenage Town Centre, but 'why' often eludes us. We can see that a neo-brutalist supermarket next door to a Georgian house is 'wrong', and we can be right for the wrong reason. The mid-19th century townscape reveals a riot of materials and architectural styles, all apparently existing happily cheek-by-jowl. Yet there were no planning constraints then.

But development has its virtues. The slums of Watford and Hitchin have departed and with them the epidemics of typhoid and cholera; infant mortality levels have plummeted, and occupational diseases are rare.

Hertford has maintained its medieval character of narrow streets, but 18th and 19th century development in the centre resulted in larger shops and house blocks than almost any other town in the county. The local photographer Arthur Elsden recorded much of the town, but it has proved difficult to date many of the images since so many of them were later reprinted as platinum prints – expensive, subtly toned and very stable – but bearing little evidence of their source. Such reprintings often remove useful data lurking on the edges of hastily mounted prints.

St Peter's Street, St Albans, around 1885. Albumen print by studio of George Washington Wilson. The Greek Revival town hall was built in 1832, a rather bright intrusion into the broad market street with its Georgian shops on the right, but with a cheerful admixture of timber-framed houses and shops too. A conspicuous triangular gable surmounts a small market infill block visible at the right, in front of the Abbey tower.

Whitehorse Street, Baldock. This is probably a wet-plate copy of a daguerreotype taken in the late 1850s. As a whole the town seems to have enjoyed a boom-and-bust existence, for in 1550 it was described as 'a market town much decayed'. By 1661 when Samuel Pepys visited the town, the market had recovered enough for him to complain 'we put in and eat a mouthfull of pork which they made us pay 14d. for, which vexed us much.'

Watford High Street, around 1865. Again, a wide street suggesting market origins, but sadly, few of the buildings of the lengthy High Street remain. In the centre an ostler attends the 'Tantivy' coach.

Stevenage High Street in 1876. In the far distance can be seen the buildings at the narrow end of the market infill so characteristic of market towns. This form of development is usually associated with broad streets in which animal sales were conducted: the infill is the fossilisation of goods stalls rather than stock stalls.

Hitchin Marketplace. Certainly a wet-plate copy of a daguerreotype like the view of Baldock, this view of the Shambles, the former butchers' area, was taken by Thomas Benwell Latchmore from the roof of his father's grocery shop in the High Street. The Italianate Corn Exchange on the right was opened in March 1853, and the Shambles were demolished by 1856 having too long already constituted an obstruction to traffic. In a thriving market town like Hitchin, traffic flow was not exactly vigorous even on market days.

The Five Horseshoes, Little Berkhampstead. Albumen print by unknown photographer around 1895. Many photographs give the impression that not much ever went on even in quite substantial towns, and to a large extent that is true.

Cricket match on the green, Harpenden, around 1870. An embodiment of the ideal of village England – perpetual summer, the click of leather on willow, no jets flying over, and no traffic.

View along Welwyn High Street, 1873. A street sweeper caught and asked to pose while, as usual, others arrive unbidden to be included.

Today, when we can categorise a street (shopping, residential, public open space) it is hard to remember that streets were not always thus. Shops in the mid-19th century were almost incidental amongst housing, which itself was a cosmopolitan entity. The wealthy lived amid the poor, and while the wealthy might be only too ready to assist the poor in particular instances, they would not in general see it as their role to equalise the disparity. Slums once formed might well remain for decades. Thorpe's Yard, Queen Street, Hitchin, 1910.

Church Street, Watford. In a situation such as this, aesthetics and practicality are always at odds. A row of shops, several hundred years old – how picturesque! But what about the occupiers? They may well see the problem in a very different way – cold, damp, verminous. As for slum clearance, the solution in many places has been for such properties to be taken into some kind of public ownership, either for preservation or for demolition.

Fishpool Street, St Albans, around the turn of the century. The cottages on the right were demolished some time between 1900 and 1905. The street as a whole was full of low-grade housing: young women declined to bring their beaux back to such squalor and, much as in Hitchin, straw-plaiting was a money-spinner, for there was a straw-hat factory further up the street on the right. Enough of this area remained by the First World War for many soldiers to be billeted there.

A view northwards along High Street, Royston, around 1890. Here the market infill on the left has been steadily renewed and the great majority of buildings appear to be Victorian, of at least two storeys. The street plan has remained the same, leaving streets of a rather intimate character.

# Work

The growth of mechanisation through the later 19th century greatly reduced the number of agricultural workers throughout Britain. They left the land and sought refuge in towns, or were attracted there by growing industries. Hertfordshire was no exception to this general movement of population, although it is in general true to say that the county was agricultural, and its industries were supported by that agriculture or closely related to it.

Throughout the county the growing of wheat, principally for local consumption, maintained the millwrights, millers and bakers, together with windmills and watermills. Many of the windmills, which reached their technological peak in the 1880s, have since burnt down or been demolished, while the watermills have been converted into attractive residences.

The growing of barley maintained both large and small breweries in most towns, together with a plethora of maltings. Watford, St Albans and Baldock retained their breweries well into the 20th century, while many others in smaller towns were gradually rationalised into larger organisations. Apart from the brewers themselves, each brewery supported coopers, making and repairing barrels, and a substantial transport fleet – drays, draymen and horses. In the south of the county, the canal network was exploited with some success, Watford utilising the Grand Junction Canal, and Hertford and Ware the Lee Navigation.

While the grain itself was utilised, the straw, then as now, was a waste product, but utilised as the raw material for the hat industry in Luton. The wives of displaced agricultural workers in many of the villages in the north west of the county plaited straw into scores of yards for a few pence a score, and sold the result to dealers from Luton, who had commissioned the particular pattern needed.

Animal waste products had been utilised for centuries – meat for food, bones for glue or light-duty tools, skins for clothing – and most towns had a tannery. The process was filthy, verminous and toxic. The skins were cleaned by knifing off remaining fat, assisted by bulldogs kept to keep down the rats. They were soaked in lime and frequently urine, to leach out the natural fats, then soaked in a solution of oak bark to tan (to attack with tannin) the fibres of the skin, and were then stuffed with other, less rancid fats to keep them supple and waterproof.

As time went on, the solidity of the social structure and of local economies meant that non-essential workers could be supported, such as newspaper printers. Starting with Victorian presses like the Albion, strong men sweated to compose and press a few hundred copies. The advent of steam and gas meant the process could be mechanised, to produce more copies in less time, and a successful printer could expand.

The change in concept from the gas engine to the Otto engine, which could be miniaturised for use in a road vehicle, was not great. Once the leap had been made, no-one could go back, and the internal combustion engine existed. Factories sprang up. Some flourished, some withered soon. In the county, several factories appeared in and around the new towns, and the Lacre works at Letchworth was a prime example. The modern world was just around the corner.

Windmill at Jack's Hill, Graveley, before 1885, when like so many windmills, it burnt down. Joseph Iredale, the miller, stands in front of the mill.

Bowman's Mill, Hitchin, 1904. The Bowman family had originally operated from a mill in Astwick in Bedfordshire, but seeing the potential of an urban mill by a railhead, they built this substantial steam powered mill in Hitchin, right beside the railway station in 1901. Extensions and additions were made on the site until it became clear that the potential of the site had become exhausted, and the site was cleared in 1986.

Workers in the yard of the King Street brewery, Watford, around 1885. Many of these men are draymen, responsible for delivery, loading and unloading the heavy oak barrels for the customer. Small breweries would contract out to local coopers, while the larger firms had resident coopers to maintain their barrels.

Group of straw plaiters in Hollow Lane, Hitchin, around 1900. While the urban plaiter lived at subsistence level, the rural plaiter was certainly no better off.

Staff of Hitchin tannery, around 1870. Tanning was an unpleasant process, removing the last vestiges of a dead animal from its skin, and then soaking the skin in lime to remove the grease. The men who worked in Russell's tannery were tough, but all suffered from plentiful warts, caused largely by the caustic solutions and indifferent hygiene.

For the wealthy, work might mean the supervision of managers for a few hours a week, or the signing of a few documents up in the City. Their sport might be to fish, to hunt, or to shoot. The keeping of game meant constant watchfulness, for game was a tempting prize for those on subsistence level and in the absence of refrigeration, fresh meat was not that easily to be had. These are the gamekeepers of Kingswalden; watchful, suspicious men who trusted none.

Typesetting the Hertfordshire Express newspaper, Exchange Yard, Hitchin 1905. Richard Hill faces the camera in the news composing room on the second floor. At this time the presses were driven through line-shafting and leather belts from a gas engine on the ground floor.

Work itself did not have to be hard to make life unpleasant. Discipline could be rigid, especially in the educational system with its obsessions for uniformity and labelling. The children here all wear the same style of garment, labelling them indisputably as girls from the orphanage. Kings Walden, around 1890.

For young women a life in service with a family could spell escape – freedom from poor and overcrowded conditions at home, even with possibilities of travel for the lucky few. It might also be a leap from the frying pan into the fire. Here four young women in service stand behind the beehives in the gardens of Walsworth House, Hitchin. 1890–1899.

The retail sector was also attractive, even in small villages such as Barley, where Mr Hagger kept his Supply Stores at the turn of the century. They sold just about everything, from apples (one penny), biscuits and cocoa to suits (from 30 shillings) not forgetting linoleum and paraffin cans on the way. Mr Hagger was keen to have his shop presentable – not only tidy provisions, but high class too: the pilasters to right and left of the display window are marbled.

# NOTICE TO THE PUBLIC.

## Early Closing of Shops

### ON THE 1st OF JULY NEXT.

The Inhabitants of Hitchin and the Neighbourhood are respectfully informed, that the Shops of the Drapers, Grocers, and others, WILL BE CLOSED FOR BUSINESS AT EIGHT O'CLOCK IN THE EVENING, on and after the 1st of July, 1850, (Saturdays excepted.)

The system of Early Closing having become general, it is hoped that it will be successfully carried out at Hitchin.

Hitchin, June 24th, 1850.

C. & T. L. PATERNOSTER, PRINTERS, HITCHIN,

Shop hours were long, though; the Hitchin Early Closing Association flourished for well over half a century, striving to inch the evening closing time of shops towards its modern level.

The rise of the factory system in the Midlands had consolidated industrial power there early in the 19th century – close initially to sources of power in the form of the coalmines. To put factories in a rural context was a laughably idealistic concept, for only later could factories grow elsewhere, when there was simple and cheap transport for the coal. That meant either canals or railways. The idealism and the economic possibility met at Letchworth. This is the stitchery room of Dent's the bookbinders in 1910.

GREAT BRITAIN'S
FOOD SUPPLY
WILL BE AMPLY
PROVIDED BY
CANADA.

COMFORTABLE
ACCOMODATION
· FOR ·
NEW SETTLERS
— AT —
CONVENIENT POINTS.

PROSPERITY
AWAITS THE SETTLER IN
CANADA.

CANADA IS DESTINED
TO BE
THE GREATEST FOOD
PRODUCING NATION.

CANADA'S
NATURAL RESOURCES,
INCLUDE
AGRICULTURE. FORESTS. MINERALS.
FRUIT AND FISH.

CANADA
WELCOMES
BRITISH SETTLERS.

As time went on and the west was slowly won, more emigrants left British shores, encouraged by propaganda such as this, displayed on a Lacre lorry built in Letchworth and with its coachwork built and fitted by Creasey's of Knebworth.

# The Studio

The early techniques of photography were two-fold: the calotype, invented by William Henry Fox Talbot, and the daguerreotype, invented by Louis Mande Daguerre. The daguerreotype produced a highly detailed though fragile image on polished silver-plated copper, an image which could be coloured by hand, but a laterally reversed image – the sitter's buttonhole appeared on the wrong side. Though this was a major drawback, especially for landscape work, the fact that only one image could be made per exposure was even greater. Processing was straightforward, though toxic. The plate was sensitised by iodine vapour, and developed with mercury vapour.

The calotype process was hedged about with licensing fees and patent restrictions, but the process itself yielded a slightly grainy image on paper, with a negative from which a potentially limitless number of copies could be simply made. Processing was simple, by immersion in relatively non-toxic liquids. The legal restrictions were the great hindrance to rapid utilisation of the method, and the daguerreotype portrait is quite common in Britain, and the calotype portrait rare.

Frederick Scott Archer – reputedly born in Bishops Stortford, though the 1851 census records his birthplace as Hertford – realised the drawbacks of the paper negative and its advantages, and set about improving it. A calotype print was made by pressing the negative against sensitised paper, and exposing this sandwich to sunlight. Since the sunlight had to penetrate the paper of the negative, it was the texture of the paper itself which gave the resulting print its characteristically grainy image.

So Archer endeavoured to replace the paper by a material called collodion, pyroxilene dissolved in ether. This was not successful – but the next stage was to coat a piece of glass with sensitised collodion. The base was now transparent, and a contact print from a glass negative was grainless. There was one drawback. The plate had to be exposed quite rapidly after coating, or its sensitivity would drop rapidly. While this was not really a drawback to studio photographers, it was to landscape photographers, and they responded by taking their darkrooms out with them. This situation continued until the discovery that gelatin was a far less volatile medium for the sensitive silver salts. A gelatin-coated plate would retain its initial sensitivity for weeks, and the photographer was thus liberated from the fixed and mobile darkroom. Plates could be loaded in special slides in the darkroom, for loading into the camera when required. Magazine cameras, holding up to twelve plates, were available from the 1880s.

This situation continued for many years, despite the fact that a patent for paper calotype roll-film had been granted as early as 1854. It took the commercial acumen of George Eastman, the founder of Kodak, and the inventiveness of Samuel N. Turner, another American, to lighten the photographer's burden. In 1892 Turner applied for a patent for a celluloid film attached at one end to a longer length of black paper. This was wound onto a flanged spool which could be loaded into a camera in daylight: film in this format can still be bought today. Eastman saw the potential of this format, and by 1894 was marketing the Bullet and the Pocket Kodak cameras to use it. Such was the success of this latter camera (the first batch of 3000 to reach Britain was sold in a few days) that by 1895 Eastman had bought up Turner's patent. The Pocket Kodak was on sale until 1900, and thereafter Eastman's success was assured. Photography was now a mass activity.

Mrs William Baker at Bayfordbury, calotype by William Robert Baker, around 1853. The first calotypes Talbot made were printed out – the exposure continued until an image appeared on the negative, which might take half an hour. Only in 1840 did Talbot discover the use of gallic acid as a developer of the invisible latent image. Exposure time to produce a usable latent image might be from a few seconds to five minutes, which made portraits practical.

Cricket match at Kings Walden. Albumen print by Thomas Benwell Latchmore, probably 1870. Detail. A charmingly informal view of the players at a country cricket match of no great pretension to style, but one which also shows the photographer's portable darkroom at the right. A large box stands on legs: the photographer gains access under the cloth which drapes the back. In such a box the glass was coated with collodion and, after the exposure had been made, developed.

Street scene at Essenden, albumen print by Thomas Benwell Latchmore. An unusually uncomposed picture, its subject matter scattered all over. But like the Kings Walden cricket match, the interesting part was quite unintentionally shown, for at the right, behind the pond, stands the photographer's van. It too has a cloth light-seal around the back. To its left lounges the photographer's assistant, leaning on a stereo camera whose twin lenses are clearly visible.

A view over Hitchin, 1866. Left half of a stereoscopic albumen print. Since two images were produced every time the negative was printed, it is not really surprising that left was often severed from right, but the image is none the less a fascinating view of a town which now sprawls to the horizon.

In the early days even the terminology was fluid; Mr Elsden of Hertford termed himself 'Photographist' on the large sign beside his studio. His glass-house is however clearly visible. Platinum print by Arthur Elsden from an earlier wet-plate negative taken around 1857.

# PORTRAIT AND LANDSCAPE PHOTOGRAPHY.

## T. B. LATCHMORE'S
# GLASS HOUSE FOR PORTRAITURE

IS NOW READY, AT

## Mr. WILLIAM DAWSON'S, BANCROFT STREET, HITCHIN.

THREE CARTES DE VISITE of each sitter are taken, for choice, but only one Portrait is guaranteed; if, however, all be approved of, a number of each can be printed.

### LIST OF PRICES:—

|  | £ | s. | d. |
|---|---|---|---|
| One Copy | | 2 | 6 |
| Six Copies | | 6 | 0 |
| Twelve Copies | | 10 | 6 |
| Twenty-five Copies | 1 | 1 | 0 |

In the construction of the Glass House special arrangements have been made for larger Portraits, and also Groups.

Specimens of Mr. Latchmore's Photography can be seen at his Rooms, Bancroft Street; also a fine Photograph of LORD DACRE'S HOUNDS, just published, copies of which are supplied by Mr. L.

Announcement of opening of Latchmore's first studio in Hitchin, in *Paternoster's Monthly Advertiser*, June 1864.

Thomas Benwell Latchmore's studio and shop in Brand Street, Hitchin, after 1870. Latchmore had his first studio in the house of a fellow-Quaker, William Dawson, but in 1870 Frederick Seebohm, a Quaker banker and philanthropist, provided the funding for a purpose-built studio beside the Town Hall. The identity of the man is not known, but it may be an assistant. Latchmore died in 1908, but was succeeded by his son Thomas William who carried on the business until his own death in 1946.

Interior of drawing room, The Grove, Watford. Albumen print by Frederick Downer. The carte-de-visite became something of a cult item, and many are visible here on either side of the fireplace, mounted en masse in display stands resembling fire-screens.

A visit to the photographer's studio was not necessarily a pleasant experience. George Avery's carte-de-visite portrait of an unknown child has a painted backdrop, but the curtain is real enough, and it crosses the floor to conceal the cast iron base of a clamp, which holds the 'victim' steady.

Samuel Bowler, the Hitchin town crier. Carte-de-visite by Thomas Benwell Latchmore. Here the clamp has been camouflaged to a large extent by a matching piece of carpet.

Here, George Hare stands determined before the camera, just before he left his work with the Great Northern Railway and emigrated to Chicago in 1872.

# Glossary of Photographic Terms Used

*Albumen print*  Paper print whose surface has been coated with egg white containing light-sensitive silver salts to render it flatter. After drying, the surface might then also be polished to give a gloss finish.

*Calotype*  Paper print with untreated surface, printed by contact with a calotype negative of waxed or unwaxed paper, yielding a characteristically grainy image.

*Collodion*  Solution of pyroxylin (a close relative of gun-cotton) in ether, invented in the 1840s as an early plastic. Used as a carrier for light-sensitive silver salts in negatives.

*Daguerreotype*  Detailed, laterally reversed image on a silvered copper plate. The image consists of microscopic lumps of mercury-silver amalgam on a silver surface, and thus is very fragile and prone to tarnishing. May or may not be hand tinted with watercolour powder colours. Always presented in a glazed wood or card case, usually of a book-like format.

*Dry-plate negative*  Glass negative with gelatine coating containing light sensitive silver salts. Maintained its sensitivity over long periods – as do modern films.

*Gelatin print*  Paper print, where the paper base is coated with an optical brightener, usually baryta (barium hydroxide), a light-sensitive layer of silver salts in gelatin, and a top gelatin layer. Used from around 1885.

*Glasshouse*  Early negatives were by modern standards insensitive and required either a lot of light or a long exposure. The long exposure was awkward for portraiture since no-one can stay totally motionless for very long, even if their head has mechanical support from a neck clamp. The glasshouse was the alternative – really little more than a greenhouse, whose glass roof allowed all available light to reach the sitter.

*Printed-out*  An image, whether calotype negative or 1920s paper print, is 'printed-out' when the exposure continues for so long that an image appears without the use of a developer. This may take some time. Fox Talbot discovered the use of gallic acid as a developer in 1840. Even a short exposure to light converts some of the silver salts even though no change is visible: the use of a developer chemically amplifies this change to render it visible. Printed-out images are brown, developed images are black, but may be converted to 'sepia' or other colours by deliberate further processing.

*Roll-film*  Negative material made of paper, cellulose nitrate (celluloid) or cellulose acetate (safety film), and sold as a continuous strip on a spool. Survives as 120 or 220 $6 \times 6$ cm film.

*Salt-paper print*  Paper coated directly with silver salts, giving a very soft, slightly furry image caused by the paper fibres poking through the image.

*Wet-plate negative*  Glass sheet coated with sensitised collodion, exposed while the collodion was still wet. Otherwise the sensitivity dropped rapidly: sometimes the wetplate was used dry for landscape work.